CW01466746

ISBN 978-1-330-92849-3
PIBN 10122592

For support please visit www.forgottenbooks.com

English
Français
Deutsche
Italiano
Español
Português

www.forgottenbooks.com

Mythology Photography **Fiction**
Fishing Christianity **Art** Cooking
Essays Buddhism Freemasonry
Medicine **Biology** Music **Ancient
Egypt** Evolution Carpentry Physics
Dance Geology **Mathematics** Fitness
Shakespeare **Folklore** Yoga Marketing
Confidence Immortality Biographies
Poetry **Psychology** Witchcraft
Electronics Chemistry History **Law**
Accounting **Philosophy** Anthropology
Alchemy Drama Quantum Mechanics
Atheism Sexual Health **Ancient History**
Entrepreneurship Languages Sport
Paleontology Needlework Islam
Metaphysics Investment Archaeology
Parenting Statistics Criminology
Motivational

Nature Poems

And Others

By

William H. Davies

Author of " The Soul's Destroyer," " New Poems,"
" Autobiography of a Super-Tramp."

London

A. C. Fifield, 44 Fleet Street, E.C.

1908

I LOVE EVERTHING
THAT IS OLD;
OLD FRIENDS, OLD TIMES,
OLD MANNERS, OLD BOOKS,
OLD WINES,

    OLIVER GOLDSMITH
      THE VICAR OF WAKEFIELD

PRINTED BY
WILLIAM BRENDON AND SON, LTD.
PLYMOUTH

Contents

D̶7̶8̶n̶

6 Contents

Nature Poems

And Others

The Muse

I HAVE no ale,
   No wine I want ;
No ornaments,
   My meat is scant.

No maid is near,
   I have no wife ;
But here's my pipe
   And, on my life :

With it to smoke,
   And woo the Muse,
To be a king
   I would not choose.

But I crave all,
   When she does fail—
Wife, ornaments,
   Meat, wine and ale.

The Rain

I HEAR leaves drinking rain;
  I hear rich leaves on top
Giving the poor beneath
   Drop after drop;
'Tis a sweet noise to hear
These green leaves drinking near.

And when the Sun comes out,
   After this rain shall stop,
A wondrous light will fill
   Each dark, round drop;
I hope the Sun shines bright;
'Twill be a lovely sight.

A Life's Love

HOW I do love to sit and dream
   Of that sweet passion, when I meet
The lady I must love for life!
  The very thought makes my Soul beat
Its wings, as though it saw that light
Silver the rims of my black night.

I see her bring a crimson mouth
 To open at a kiss, and close ;
I see her bring her two fair cheeks,
 That I may paint on each a rose ;
I see her two hands, like doves white,
Fly into mine and hide from sight.

In fancy hear her soft, sweet voice ;
 My eager Soul, to catch her words,
Waits at the ear, with Noah's haste
 To take God's message-bearing Birds ;
What passion she will in me move—
That Lady I for life must love !

Robin Redbreast

R OBIN on a leafless bough,
 Lord in Heaven, how he sings !
Now cold Winter's cruel Wind
 Makes playmates of poor, dead things.

How he sings for joy this morn !
 How his breast doth pant and glow !
Look you how he stands and sings,
 Half-way up his legs in snow !

If these crumbs of bread were pearls,
 And I had no bread at home,
He should have them for that song ;
 Pretty Robin Redbreast, Come.

Tyrants

PEACE makes more slaves than savage War,
  Since tyrants, backed by their Land's Law—
Needing no deadly armament—
Can force a people to consent
To toil like slaves for little pay,
In shops and factories all day ;
Make human moles, that sweat and slave
In dark, cold, cheerless rooms ; who have
No blood, to make them well again,
If foul Disease should give them pain.
The cold, proud rich they, without cares,
In comfort live ; like surly bears
That eat and sleep in caves of ice
The Heavenly Sun has painted nice ;
Tyrants that would, to have their rent,
Turn tenants' Christmas into Lent,
For fast instead of feast.   What, free !
When masters, who hate Liberty,
Can in their height of power and greed
Force weaker men to serve their need ?
Dogs may rear cats, the cat a rat,
And wolves stay hunger, loving what
They could devour—so masters may
Make men their care instead of prey.
The Fly has many eyes : I guess
A Spider can see more with less :
One Tyrant, though not right, is strong
To punish thousands for no wrong.

To a Butterfly

WE have met,
　　You and I;
Loving man,
　　Lovely Fly.

If I thought
　　You saw me,
And love made
　　You so free

To come close—
　　I'd not move
Till you tired
　　Of my love.

The Milkmaid's Call

AS I walked down a lane this morn,
　　I heard a sweet voice cry, Come, Come!
And then I saw ten dull, fat cows
　　Begin to race like horses home;
Like horses in their pace,
Though lacking horses' grace.

That voice, which did uplift those feet
　　Of cows, uplifted mine likewise;
For, with a heart so light, I walked
　　Until the sweat did blind my eyes;
And all the way back home,
I heard her cry, Come, Come!

The Wind

SOMETIMES he roars among the leafy trees
  Such sounds as in a narrow cove, when Seas
Rush in between high rocks; or grandly roll'd,
Like music heard in churches very old.
Sometimes he makes the children's happy sound,
When they play hide and seek, and one is found.
Sometimes he whineth like a dog in sleep,
Bit by the merciless, small fleas; then deep
And hollow sounds come from him, as starved men
Oft hear rise from their empty parts; and then
He'll hum a hollow groan, like one sick lain,
Who fears a move will but increase his pain.
And now he makes an awful wail, as when
From dark coal-pits are brought up crushed, dead men
    men
To frantic wives. When he's on mischief bent,
He breeds more ill than that strange Parliament
Held by the witches, in the Hebrides;
He's here, he's there, to do what'er he please.
For well he knows the spirits' tricks at night,
Of slamming doors, and blowing out our light,
And tapping at our windows, rattling pails,
And making sighs and moans, and shouts and wails.
'Twas he no doubt made that young man's hair white,
    white,
Who slept alone in a strange house one night,
And was an old man in the morn and crazed,
And all who saw and heard him were amazed.

Jenny

NOW I grow old, and flowers are weeds,
  I think of days when weeds were flowers;
When Jenny lived across the way,
  And shared with me her childhood hours.

Her little teeth did seem so sharp,
  So bright and bold, when they were shown,
You'd think if passion stirred her she
  Could bite and hurt a man of stone.

Her curls, like golden snakes, would lie
  Upon each shoulder's front, as though
To guard her face on either side—
  They raised themselves when Winds did blow.

How sly they were! I could not see,
  Nor she feel them begin to climb
Across her lips, till there they were,
  To be forced back time after time.

If I could see an Elm in May
  Turn all his dark leaves into pearls,
And shake them in the light of noon—
  That sight had not shamed Jenny's curls.

And, like the hay, I swear her hair
  Was getting golder every day;
Yes, golder when 'twas harvested,
  Under a bonnet stacked away.

Ah, Jenny's gone, I know not where ;
  Her face I cannot hope to see ;
And every time I think of her
  The world seems one big grave to me.

Sweet Youth

AND art thou gone, sweet Youth ?   Say Nay !
  For dost thou know what power was thine,
That thou couldst give vain shadows flesh,
  And laughter without any wine,
From the heart fresh ?

And art thou gone, sweet Youth ?   Say Nay !
  Not left me to Time's cruel spite ;
He'll pull my teeth out one by one,
  He'll paint my hair first grey, then white,
He'll scrape my bone.

And art thou gone, sweet Youth ?   Alas !
  For ever gone ! I know it well ;
Earth has no atom, nor the sky,
  That has not thrown the kiss Farewell—
Sweet Youth, Good-Bye !

Nature's Friend

SAY what you like,
  All things love me !
I pick no flowers—
  That wins the Bee.

The Summer's Moths
  Think my hand one—
To touch their wings—
  With Wind and Sun.

The garden Mouse
  Comes near to play ;
Indeed, he turns
  His eyes away.

The Wren knows well
  I rob no nest ;
When I look in,
  She still will rest.

The hedge stops Cows,
  Or they would come
After my voice
  Right to my home.

The Horse can tell,
  Straight from my lip,
My hand could not
  Hold any whip.

Say what you like,
All things love me l
Horse, Cow, and Mouse,
Bird, Moth and Bee.

A Maiden and her Hair

HER cruel hands go in and out,
  Like two pale woodmen working there,
To make a nut-brown thicket clear—
  The full, wild foliage of her hair.

Her hands now work far up the North,
  Then, fearing for the South's extreme,
They into her dark waves of hair
  Dive down so quick—it seems a dream.

They're in the light again with speed,
  Tossing the loose hair to and fro,
Until, like tamèd snakes, the coils
  Lie on her bosom in a row.

For wise inspection, up and down
  One coil her busy hands now run ;
To screw and twist, to turn and shape,
  And here and there to work like one.

And **now,** those white hands, still like **one,**
   Are working at the perilous end ;
Where they must knot those nut-brown coils,
   Which will hold fast, though still they'll bend.

Sometimes one hand must fetch strange tools,
   The other then must work alone ;
But when more instruments are brought,
   See both make up the time that's gone.

Now that her hair is bound secure,
   Coil top of coil, in smaller space,
Ah, now I see how smooth her brow,
   And her simplicity of face.

Sweet Music

A H, Music ! it doth sound more sweet
   Than rain on crispèd leaves ; or when
Beauty doth stroke a kitten rose,
   And screams, to feel her fingers then
Scratched by its little claws.

Drowned, Music, in thy waves, I saw
   My whole long Past before me go ;
Now, rouse me with a merry shout—
   Such as charm children, when Winds blow
The light they love clean out.

B

Early Morn

Laugh thee, sweet Music, like those girls,
  When each was fit, but none were wed ;
As they did banter a shy boy,
  Who could not raise on high his head
And face their wicked joy.

Early Morn

WHEN I did wake this morn from sleep,
  It seemed I heard birds in a dream ;
Then I arose to take the air—
  The lovely air that made birds scream ;
Just as a green hill launched the ship
Of gold, to take its first clear dip.

And it began its journey then,
  As I came forth to take the air ;
The timid Stars had vanished quite,
  The Moon was dying with a stare ;
Horses, and kine, and sheep were seen
As still as pictures, in fields green.

It seemed as though I had surprised
  And trespassed in a golden world
That should have passed while men still slept !
  The joyful birds, the ship of gold,
The horses, kine and sheep did seem
As they would vanish for a dream.

The Battle

THERE was a battle in her face,
  Between a Lily and a Rose :
,My Love would have the Lily win
  And I the Lily lose.

I saw with joy that strife, first one,
  And then the other uppermost ;
Until the Rose roused all its blood,
  And then the Lily lost.

When she's alone, the Lily rules,
  By her consent, without mistake :
But when I come that red Rose leaps
  To battle for my sake.

A Beggar's Life

WHEN farmers sweat and toil at ploughs,
  Their wives give me cool milk and sweet ;
When merchants in their office brood,
  Their ladies give me cakes to eat,
And hot tea for my happy blood ;
  This is a jolly life indeed,
  To do no work and get my need.

I have no child for future thought,
   I feed no belly but my own,
And I can sleep when toilers fail;
   Content, though sober, sleeps on stone,
But Care can't sleep with down and ale;
   This is a happy life indeed,
   To do no work and get my need.

I trouble not for pauper's grave,
   There is no feeling after death;
The king will be as deaf to praise   .
   As I to blame—when this world saith
A word of us in after days;
   It is a jolly life indeed,
   To do no work and get my need.

The Moth

SAY, silent Moth,
      Why thou hast let
The midnight come,
      And no dance yet.

Man's life is years,
      Thy life a day;
Is thine too long
      To be all play?

Man's life is long,
    He lives for years;
So long a time
    Breeds many fears.

Thy life is short:
    What'er its span,
Life's worth seems small
    Be't Moth or Man.

Day's Black Star

IS it that small black star,
    Twinkling in broad daylight,
Upon the bosom of
    Yon clouds so white—
Is it that small black thing
Makes earth and all Heaven ring!

Sing, you black star; and soar
    Until, alas! too soon
You fall to earth in one
    Long singing swoon;
But you will rise again
To heaven, from this green plain.

Sing, sing, sweet star; though black,
    Your company's more bright
Than any star that shines
    With a white light;
Sing, Skylark, sing; and give
To me thy joy to live.

Go, Angry One

GO, angry One, and let tears cold
    Put out the fires thine eyes now hold;
Let those dark clouds, that make my pain,
Clear themselves pure with thine eyes' rain;
Let Thy cheeks' roses, that once stood
Unblemished by wild Passion's blood,
Be washed by thee in penance dew,
To gain back their first happy hue;
Recover thy voice, sweet and low,
That has such little music now.
But let not anger frost, and kill
The trembling flowers of Love that will
Come pleading unto you for me—
Which would for both great pity be.
Go, angry Beauty, and get calm;
And, when thou art all spent of harm,
Look how I come with greater love;
And anger once again will move
Thee, my wild Pet—but not so strong
That you will think my kisses wrong.

Dead Born

A PERFECT child, with hands and feet,
    With heart and bones;
Which no man's hand could fashion out
    Of clay or stones.

Yet this, Alas ! is but cold clay ;
    The mortal breath
Is lacking, for this perfect child
    Is born in death.

Oft have I seen its mother's joy—
    A new-made wife ;
And knew she fed on secret hope
    For her child's life.

And now her heart breaks ; she can hear
    No sweet cries wild ;
There needs no joyful soothing for
    Her dead-born child.

The Change

NOW Winter's here ; he and his ghostly Winds
    That day and night swing on the branches
      bare.
There's February, with his weak, running eyes,
And dog-like nose, that's always damp and cold.
November, who doth make Heaven like one cloud ;
And, if he shines at all, his sunsets are
A ghastly white ; no sound of birds—save, now
And then, a pheasant hiccups like a child.
There's cold December too ; he takes the Brook,
And lodges him in a strong tomb of ice—

The last sweet voice that Nature charms us with.
I cannot help but think of Autumn now,
Ere any leaves begin to fall, and when
He made the dark and sullen forest smile,
And gave the trees gold tresses for their dark;
And was, as I have heard, so generous
That men could feed their pigs on his rich fruit.
And I go farther back: how Spring did clothe
The aged Oak—whose four tremendous arms
Might well be bodies of still noble trees.
And how Spring's sparkling meadows stormed the
      Clouds   .
With little black balls that went singing up;
And how rain-arrows struck the earth so hard,
Giving no wound to little Leaves and Buds,
But only tickling them to laugh and dance.
And I think too of Summer in her prime—
The tidal wave of Summer's yellow fields;
And her gold tresses, cut and loose on earth,
With merry men and women there all day
Laughing and combing them; when Swallows
      made
Bewildering dives of forty feet and more;
And Winds sang only loud enough in trees
To give Love confidence for whispering.
And now the world's so bare and cold by day:
It seems but yesterday I welcomed Night
That she hung out her silver orb so cool,
In place of Day's red danger-lamp, which forced
Me into shade all day.

A Richer Freight

YOU Nightingales, that came so far,
    From Afric's shore ;
With these rich notes, unloaded now
    Against my door ;

Most true they are far richer freight
    Than ships can hold ;
That come from there with ivory tusks,
    And pearls, and gold.

But you'll return more rich, sweet birds,
    By many notes ;
When you take my Love's sweeter ones
    Back in your throats,

And Afric's coast will be enriched
    By how you sing !
What ! you'll bring others back with you,
    To learn—next Spring.

School's Out

GIRLS scream,
    Boys shout ;
Dogs bark,
    School's out.

Cats run,
   Horses shy ;
Into trees
   Birds fly.

Babes wake
   Open-eyed ;
If they can,
   Tramps hide.

Old man,
   Hobble home ;
Merry mites,
   Welcome.

A Happy Life

O WHAT a life is this I lead,
   Far from the hum of human greed ;
Where Crows, like merchants dressed in black,
Go leisurely to work and back ;
Where Swallows leap and dive and float,
And Cuckoo sounds his cheerful note ;
Where Skylarks now in clouds do rave,
Half mad with fret that their souls have
By hundreds far more joyous notes
Than they can manage with their throats.

The ploughman's heavy horses run
The field as if in fright—for fun,
Or stand and laugh in voices shrill;
Or roll upon their backs until
The sky's kicked small enough—they think;
Then to a pool they go and drink.
The kine are chewing their old cud,
Dreaming, and never think to add
Fresh matter that will taste—as they
Lie motionless, and dream away.

I hear the sheep a-coughing near;
Like little children, when they hear
Their elders' sympathy—so these
Sheep force their coughs on me, and please;
And many a pretty lamb I see,
Who stops his play on seeing me,
And runs and tells his mother then.
Lord, who would live in towns with men,
And hear the hum of human greed—
With such a life as this to lead.

The Sweetest Dream

NAY, no more bitterness from me;
   The past is gone, so let it be;
And I will keep smiles softer than
The sad smiles of a dying man
For a child comforter—to give
My sweetest dream, that still must live.

My sweetest dream, that comes more bold ;
Of one sweet, simple child of old ;
Who, though a queen, and a great one,
Would wear her jewels like a nun ;
When miser leaves unlocked his door,
I may forget her—not before.

City and Country

THE City has dull eyes,
    The City's cheeks are pale ;
The City has black spit,
    The City's breath is stale.

The Country has red cheeks,
    The Country's eyes are bright ;
The Country has sweet breath,
    The Country's spit is white.

Dull eyes, breath stale ; ink spit
    And cheeks like chalk—for thee ;
Eyes bright, red cheeks ; sweet breath
    And spit like milk—for me.

The One Real Gem

WEALTH, Power, and Fame—aye, even Love,
 Are but an hour's delight, and go ;
But Sleep's a blessing to hold fast
 Till her warm dew becomes Death's snow ;
All men that scorned Sleep in the past,
 For any thing beneath the Sun,
 Will rue it ere their life be done.

Much it perplexed of late to know
 What made my heart with joy so light ;
Until I thought of how sweet Sleep
 Did, for so many hours each night,
Keep me in her delicious deep :
 Charmed me each night with her sweet powers,
 In one unbroken stretch of hours.

All-powerful Sleep, thou canst give slaves
 Kings for attendants ; and their straw
Becomes in thy soft hands like down ;
 Thou one real gem, without a flaw,
That purely shineth in Life's crown ;
 For Wealth, and Power, and Fame are paste,
 That into common ashes waste.

Joy and Pleasure

NOW, Joy is born of parents poor,
  And Pleasure of our richer kind ;
Though Pleasure's free, she cannot sing
  As sweet a song as Joy confined.

Pleasure's a Moth, that sleeps by day
  And dances by false glare at night ;
But Joy's a Butterfly, that loves
  To spread its wings in Nature's light.

Joy's like a Bee that gently sucks
  Away on blossoms its sweet hour ;
But Pleasure's like a greedy Wasp,
  That plums and cherries would devour.

Joy's like a Lark that lives alone,
  Whose ties are very strong, though few ;
But Pleasure like a Cuckoo roams,
  Makes much acquaintance, no friends true.

Joy from her heart doth sing at home,
  With little care if others hear ;
But Pleasure then is cold and dumb,
  And sings and laughs with strangers near.

A Merry Hour

AS long as I see Nature near,
   I will, when old, cling to life dear :
E'en as the old dog holds so fast
With his three teeth, which are his last.
For Lord, how merry now am I !
Tickling with straw the Butterfly,
Where she doth in her clean, white dress,
Sit on a green leaf, motionless,
To hear Bees hum away the hours.
I shake those Bees too off the Flowers,
So that I may laugh soft to hear
Their hoarse resent and angry stir.
I hear the sentry Chanticleer
Challenge each other far and near,
From farm to farm, and it rejoices
Me this hour to mock their voices ;
There's one red Sultan near me now,
Not all his wives make half his row.
Cuckoo ! Cuckoo ! was that a bird,
Or but a mocking boy you heard ?
You heard the Cuckoo first, 'twas he ;
The second time—Ha, ha ! 'twas Me.

Love's Birth

I HEARD a voice methought was sweet;
  Skylark, I mused, thy praise is done;
That voice I'd rather hear than thine
  With twenty songs in one.

And she, in sooth, is fair, thought I,
  Looking at her with cold, calm eyes—
As the Lily at May's feet, or Rose
  That on June's bosom lies.

I heard one day a step; a voice,
  Heard in a room next door to mine;
And then, I heard long, laughing peals,
  For *him!* from Rosaline.

Again she laughs; what, mocking me?
  I shook like coward in the night—
Who fears to either lie in dark
  Or rise to make a light.

For weeks I cursed the day I met
  That fair sleep-robber, Rosaline;
Till Love came pure from smoke and flame—
  I swore she should be mine.

And in her house I held her firm,
  She closed her eyes and lay at rest;
But still she laughed, as if a bird
  Should sing in its warm nest.

Nature's Moods

I LIKE the showers that make the grass so fresh,
  And birds' notes fresher too ; and like the Mist,
Who makes thin shadows of those heavy hills,
That carried in the light a hundred fields,
A score of woods, and many a house of stone.
Or see the jealous Sun appear, and make
That Mist, Morn's phantom lover, go ;
And drive him to the farthest hill in sight,
On which he'll make his last and dying stand ;
A lover, he ? Ah, no ; a vampire, who
Comes out of Night's black grave to suck Morn's
    blood.
I like to see the Sun appear at last,
To meet the Clouds, Clouds armed with arrow-
    rain ;
And see him lift his rainbow banner high.
Or see upon a misty night how Stars
Half ope their eyes and close, as if in doubt
To keep awake or not ; how sometimes they
Do seem so far and faint, I almost think
My eyes play false, and they are Fancy's stars.
I welcome Nature in her every mood :
To see a hundred crows toss wild about,
Blowing in Heaven's face like balls of soot,
As they make their delirious cries, sure signs
Of coming storm—not half a one, I hope.

Truly Great

MY walls outside must have some flowers,
   My walls within must have some books ;
A house that's small ; a garden large,
   And in it leafy nooks.

A little gold that's sure each week ;
   That comes not from my living kind,
But from a dead man in his grave,
   Who cannot change his mind.

A lovely wife, and gentle too ;
   Contented that no eyes but mine
Can see her many charms, nor voice
. To call her beauty fine.

Where she would in that stone cage live,
   A self-made prisoner, with me ;
While many a wild bird sang around,
   On gate, on bush, on tree.

And she sometimes to answer them,
   In her far sweeter voice than all ;
Till birds, that loved to look on leaves,
   Will doat on a stone wall.

With this small house, this garden large,
   This little gold, this lovely mate,
With health in body, peace at heart—
   Show me a man more great.

A Familiar Voice

A H, what fond memories that voice doth bring !
   Even to strangers sweet : no others sing
Their common speech, like men of Cambria's race ;
How much more sweet to me then was that voice !
It filled me with sweet memories ; as when
I heard one hum the March of Harlech Men,
Dying, five thousand miles from home ! Now we
Lived in a city dark, where Poverty,
More hard than rocks, and crueller than foam,
Keeps many a great Ulysses far from home,
With neither kings nor gods to help him forth.
Tell me, sweet voice, what part of that dear earth
Thou callest thine ? I asked, to please my whim :
His answer could not cool my pride in him.
For Wales is Wales ; one patriotic flame
From North to South, from East to West the same ;
There is no difference in our Cymric breed
Of Highlander and Lowlander ; no creed
Can enter there to make their hearts divide ;
Nay, Wales is Wales throughout, and of one pride.
So, in that city, by stone walls confined,
We of our native land spake with one mind.
We could breathe in vast spaces there : the eye
Could lead proud Fancy in captivity
Mile after mile adown the valleys long,
The kindest hearts in all the world among.
One woman's tears could moisten all the land,
As in that very hour was known : band upon band
Of Cymry swarming from their collieries
To search the hills, in hours of sleep and ease,

For one lost child ; a woman's grief could claim
The fiery hearts that tyrants ne'er could tame.
The noblest hearts on earth are in those hills,
For they make national their local ills ;
Theirs are the hearts of oak, in truth they are,
So soft in peace, yet knotted hard in war ;
Of such an oak as, smoothèd down by Pain,
Shows flowers of Pity deep in its clear grain.
We did compare this City dame with neat
And simple Jenny Jones, with her charms sweet
As are shy berries under shady leaves,
Hiding from light to sweeten of themselves ;
This City dame, with plumes and satin trail—
An empty craft that carries finer sail
Than one whose hull is full of pearls and gold ;
For, save in song, our Jenny is not bold.
And so we talked till, with an oath, we swore
We would return and never wander more.

A Summer's Noon

WHITE lily clouds
    In violet skies ;
The Sun is at
    His highest rise.

The Bee doth hum,
    Every bird sings ;
The Butterflies
    Full stretch their wings.

Life

The Brook doth dance
  To his own song ;
The Hawthorn now
  Smells sweet and strong.

The green Leaves clap
  Their wings to fly ;
Like Birds whose feet
  Bird lime doth tie.

Sing all you Birds,
  Hum all you Bees ;
Clap your green wings,
  Leaves on the trees—

I'm one with all,
  This present hour :
Things-far-away
  Have lost their power.

Life

ALONE beneath Heaven's roof I stand ;
  It is a cold and frosty night ;
Big, spider stars, with many legs,
  Upon Heaven's ceiling spin in sight ;
I hear afar the homeless Wind,
  Carrying abroad her wailing child
That, when she hurries faster, screams
  The louder and more wild.

Now thoughts of Life make me feel sick;
  No other joy on earth, it seems,
Than to pursue our quest for some
  False Eldorado of our dreams;
Pale Fear doth like a spider pull,
  Sucking my heart; it seems I grow
A man of feathers and light down,
  And cold winds through me blow.

For Life seems empty of all worth;
  No wisdom in the morning shows
The day its duty; yet each night
  Is wise to show us its vain close.
Time's hours are precious—What! To whom?
  Is there one man has faith at night
That he has bought true worth with them,
  And spent his day aright?

In Days Gone

I HAD a sweet companion once,
  And in the meadows we did roam;
And in the one-star night returned
  Together home.

When Bees did roar like midget bulls,
  Or quietly rob nodding Flowers—
We two did roam the fields so green,
  In Summer hours.

She like the Rill did laugh, when he
    Plays in the quiet woods alone ;
She was as red as Summer's rose—
    The first one blown.

Her hair as soft as any moss
    , That running water still keeps wet ;
And her blue eye—it seemed as if
    A Violet

Had in a Lily's centre grown,
    To see the blue, and white around—
'Twas tender as the Glowworm's light
    On a lost mound.

And, like the face of a sweet well
    Buried alive in a stone place—
So calm, so fresh, so soft, so bright
    Was that child's face.

March

THERE'S not one leaf can say to me
    It shines with this year's greenery.
A stoat-like Wind, without a sound,
Doth creep and startle from the ground
The brown leaves, and they fly about,
And settle, till again found out.
But Spring, for very sure, is born :
E'en though I see, this misty morn,

The face of Phœbus cold and white,
As hers who sits his throne at night ;
For I can hear how birds—not bold
Enough to sing full songs—do scold
Their timid hearts to make a try.
The unseen hand of Spring doth lie
Warm on my face ; the air is sweet
And calm ; it has a pleasant heat
That makes my two hands swell, as though
They had gloves on.   Spring makes no show
Of leaves and blossoms yet, but she
Has worked upon this blood in me ;
And everything of flesh I meet
Can feel, it seems, her presence sweet.

The Laughers

MARY and Maud have met at the door,
    Oh, now for a din ;   I told you so :
They're laughing at once with sweet, round mouths,
    Laughing for what ? does anyone know ?

Is it known to the bird in the cage,
    That shrieketh for joy his high top notes,
After a silence so long and grave—
    What started at once those two sweet throats ?

Is it known to the Wind that he takes
    Advantage at once and comes right in ?
Is it known to the cock in the yard,
    That crows—the cause of that merry din ?

Is it known to the babe that he shouts?
  Is it known to the old, purring cat?
Is it known to the dog, that he barks
  For joy—what Mary and Maud laugh at?

Is it known to themselves? It is not,
  But beware of their great shining eyes;
For Mary and Maud will soon, I swear,
  Find a cause to make far merrier cries.

The Thieves

THIEVES, Death and Absence, come
  No more to my heart's home:
Behold my chambers bare,
I make no thing my care.

As fast as I aught bring
In place of stolen thing,
One of ye two doth come
Again to my heart's home.

Henceforth I'll leave it bare,
Cold winds shall enter there;
For nothing keep I can—
Of plant, or beast, or man.

Solitude

YES, Solitude indeed : for I can see
   Trees all around and, to the west of me—
So near I could almost throw there a stone—
A mountain and a forest stand in one !
I've watched that mountain-top an hour and more,
To see some bird-discoverer sail o'er
That mighty wave of earth and settle here—
For to go back that way he would not dare.
And, did I see that bird, 'twould give such joy
As in days gone, when I, a little boy,
Saw lying in a dock the ten-foot boat
That did across the deep Atlantic float ;
With one old man, who strapped himself fast down
Three days and nights, knowing that he must drown,
If once a Wind or Wave could lift him free.
Yes, this is Solitude, for I can see
Nothing around but mountains and their trees,
And all the sweet flowers close, and birds, and bees.
The bees, that drink from tankards every size,
Colour and shape, do heave no feeble sighs,
But murmur loud their praise ; and every bird
Sang sweet—till but a moment since they heard
A Blackbird's startled shriek, when suddenly
He saw me motionless beneath a tree,
And made them dumb in leaves and out ; and made
Even tame Robin look around, afraid.
I see a house or two adown the lane,
But no sign there of human life ; in vain
The Cuckoo makes his strange but cheerful note,
To get an answer sweet from Childhood's throat.

In this green valley, deep and silent, roam
Cattle that seem to have no other home,
Nor dream of any from their open vale.
And now I see a wall and gate, so stale
And old—black without paint ; which seems to me
Could tell some sweet, half dreadful history.
And then I walked and saw a field close by,
And what was seen there opened wide my eye ;
A man with a white horse and, this I swear,
Both of them in their sleep were ploughing there.
Then home I went and, till I reached that place,
I never saw another mortal's face.
A week here now ; not one hard living tramp,
Of England's many, finds this quiet camp,
To cheat with ready lies and solemn looks
Me, when a dreamer I come straight from books ;
And still I would with gladness, now and then,
Be cheated by those happy, wandering men.

Australian Bill

AUSTRALIAN BILL is dying fast,
  For he's a drunken fool :
He either sits in an alehouse,
  Or stands outside a school.

He left this house of ours at seven,
  And he was drunk by nine ;
And when I passed him near a school
  He nods his head to mine.

The Boy

When Bill took to the hospital,
  Sick, money he had none—
He came forth well, but lo ! his home,
  His wife and child had gone.

'I'll watch a strange school every day,
  Until the child I see ;
For Liz will send the child to school—
  No doubt of that,' says he.

And 'Balmy' Tom is near as bad,
  A-drinking ale till blind :
No absent child grieves he, but there's
  A dead love on his mind.

But Bill, poor Bill, is dying fast,
  For he's the greater fool ;
He either sits in an alehouse
  Or stands outside a school.

The Boy

GO, little boy,
  Fill thee with joy ;
For Time gives thee
Unlicensed hours,
  To run in fields,
And roll in flowers.

A little boy
Can life enjoy ;
   If but to see
The horses pass,
   When shut indoors
Behind the glass.

Go, little boy,
Fill thee with joy ;
   Fear not, like man,
The kick of wrath,
   That you do lie
In some one's path.

Time is to thee
Eternity,
   As to a bird
Or butterfly ;
   And in that faith
True joy doth lie.

A Swallow that flew into the room

I GIVE thee back thy freedom, bird,
  But know, I am amazed to see
These lovely feathers, which thou hast
  Concealed so many years from me.

46   A Lovely Woman

Oft have I watched thee cut the name
    Of Summer in the clear, blue air,
And praised thy skilful lettering—
    But never guessed thou wert so fair.

It is, maybe, thou hast no wish
    For praise save for thy works of grace :
Thou scornest beauty, like the best
    And wisest of our human race.

A Lovely Woman

NOW I can see what Helen was :
    Men cannot see this woman pass
And be not stirred ; as Summer's Breeze
Sets leaves in battle on the trees.
A woman moving gracefully,
With golden hair enough for three,
Which, mercifully l is not loose,
But lies in coils to her head close ;
With lovely eyes, so dark and blue,
So deep, so warm, they burn me through.
I see men follow her, as though
Their homes were where her steps should go.
She seemed as sent to our cold race
For fear the beauty of her face
Made Paradise in flames like Troy—
I could have gazed all day with joy.
In fancy I could see her stand
Before a savage, fighting band,

And make them, with her words and looks,
Exchange their spears for shepherds' crooks,
And sing to sheep in quiet nooks;
In fancy saw her beauty make
A thousand gentle priests uptake
Arms for her sake, and shed men's blood.
The fairest piece of womanhood,
Lovely in feature, form and grace,
I ever saw, in any place.

Money

WHEN I had money, money, O!
    I knew no joy till I went poor;
For many a false man as a friend
    Came knocking all day at my door.

Then felt I like a child that holds
    A trumpet that he must not blow
Because a man is dead; I dared
    Not speak to let this false world know.

Much have I thought of life, and seen
    How poor men's hearts are ever light;
And how their wives do hum like bees
    About their work from morn till night.

So, when I hear these poor ones laugh,
    And see the rich ones coldly frown—
Poor men, think I, need not go up
    So much as rich men should come down.

48 **The Cheat**

When I had money, money, O !
My many friends proved all untrue ;
But now I have no money, O l
My friends are real, though very few.

The Cheat

YES, let the truth be heard,
Bacchus, you rosy cheat :
That you do rob this world
Of pictures and songs sweet ;
You give men dreams, 'tis true,
But take their will to do.

You send them sleep as kings—
They wake as trembling slaves ;
Sent singing to their beds,
They rise like ghosts from graves ;
They drink to get will power—
Then wait a sober hour.

They shake, like leaves with stems
Part broken on a tree ;
As bees from flower to flower,
Men go from spree to spree ;
Until their days are run,
And not one sweet task done.

Where we differ

TO think my thoughts all hers,
    Not one of hers is mine ;
She laughs—while I must sigh ;
    She sings—while I must whine.

She eats—while I must fast ;
    She reads—while I am blind ;
She sleeps—while I must wake ;
    Free—I no freedom find.

To think the world for me
    Contains but her alone,
And that her eyes prefer
    Some ribbon, scarf, or stone.

When I returned

WHEN I returned to that great London Town,
    And saw Old Father Thames, one August
        night,
Looking at me with half a thousand eyes ;
    When I at morn saw how the Heavenly light
Could burnish that dull gold on dome and spire—
I lost all instinct, like a horse near fire.

D

No thought of ragged youths, and ghastly girls
   Whose metal laughter oft had pained my ear,
For many a pleasant hour ; but soon, Alas !
   So shaken was my mind by Traffic's stir,
I felt an impulse mad to shriek out loud,
As if my voice could quiet that vast crowd.

Soon saw how false that empty glitter was,
   For men did drop of hunger there, and die ;
There I saw many a homeless man, with death
   The silver lining to his cloud—then I
Saw woolly sheep, fat cows in meadows green,
In place of such men ragged, pale and lean.

The Daisy

I KNOW not why thy beauty should
   Remind me of the cold, dark grave—
Thou Flower, as fair as Moonlight, when
   She kissed the mouth of a black Cave.

All other Flowers can coax the Bees,
   All other Flowers are sought but thee :
Dost thou remind them all of Death,
   Sweet Flower, as thou remindest me ?

Thou seemest like a blessèd ghost,
   So white, so cold, though crowned with gold ;
Among these glazèd Buttercups,
   And purple Thistles, rough and bold.

When I am dead, nor thought of more,
   Out of all human memory—
Grow you on my forsaken grave,
   And win for me a stranger's sigh.

A day or two the lilies fade ;
   A month, aye less, no friends are seen :
Then, claimant to forgotten graves,
   Share my lost place with the wild green.

A Vagrant's Life

WHAT art thou, Life, and what am I ?
   Here, every day that passes by
Doth prove an idle, empty cheat ;
And hint at some false scheme to meet
The coming day and get more mirth—
Which will pass by with no more worth.
I fear to give one thing my heart,
That Death or Absence may us part ;
And 'tis a misery to live
Alone, and have much love to give.
I envy oft that vagrant poor :
He has no landlady next door ;

For beauty he has ne'er a care—
More happy bald than with much hair ;
He has no child to save gold for,
No patriot's love calls him to war ;
No house to burn, no ship to sink,
No wish for fame ; no cause to think
Of landlord, rent, or decent cloth ;
No wish for Pleasure's hall : in sooth,
With a plain crust, the Sun o'erhead,
Some straw at night to make his bed,
And drinking water, on his knee,
That is the life for him—and me.

A Luckless Pair

POOR, luckless Bee, this sunny morn ;
   That in the night a Wind and Rain
Should strip this Apple-tree of bloom,
   And make it green again.

You, luckless Bee, must now seek far
   For honey on the windy leas ;
No sheltered garden, near your hive,
   To fill a bag with ease.

My Love was like this Apple-tree,
   In one sweet bloom, all yesterday ;
But something changed her too, Alas !
   And I am turned away.

The Trickster

WHEN first I left a town,
    And lived in Nature's parts,
I heard the march of men,
    And whistles, horses, carts;
And it to me did seem
Nature was but a dream.

I heard blows struck outside,
    And bodies fall all day,
And laughter, shrieks, and groans;
    And who, think you, did play
These mad pranks on my mind?
It was the merry Wind.

He blubbered oft near by,
    Against the corner stone;
Like sulking child, who'll not
    Come in, nor yet be gone—
To whom full well 'tis known
His mother's home alone.

The Two Lives

YOUTH thinks green apples sweet,
    Age thinks red cherries sour;
Age calls a flower a weed,
    Youth calls a weed a flower.

Youth thinks the world is large,
  But Age doth think it small;
Youth walks on stilts, but Age
  Fears, on his feet, to fall.

Youth claims eternal life,
  With hours, too long to sum;
Age counts his few hours gone,
  And fewer hours to come.

Age sits and feebly chirps,
  But Youth does dance and sing;
Age is Time's pensioner,
  Youth is Time's king—his king!

Beauty's Danger

HOW can she safely walk this earth,
    And not be robbed of all her worth,
By bulls and bees that may catch sight
Of her lips waving their red light.
Birds could make bedding of her hair,
And her ripe lips could tempt wasps there;
If Summer's moths should see her eyes,
They'd drop on them, and never rise,
But, filled at once with mad desire,
Would soon put out those lamps of fire,
With their lives sacrificed : no gem
Shines on Night's ebon breast like them.

Even the hawk a foe might prove,
To see her bosom in a move ;
And thinking there she hid young mice,
Or·birds, that would not sleep in peace.
For never doth that bosom rest ;
If she doth hold her breath, there must
Follow a storm ; the only boat
'That ever on that sea did float
Is this blessed hand of mine : when I
As helpless as a boat must lie—
When seamaids' music makes the Breeze
Drop on the sails and sleep.   O she's
An everlasting spring, that flows
When all my other springs do close.

Childhood's Hours

MY heart's a coffin cold,
  In which my Childhood lies
Unburied yet ; and will—
  Until this body dies.

I think me every hour
  Of those sweet, far-off days
That draw so very close,
  And show their pretty ways.

Where'er I am they come,
  Those ghosts, my Childhood Hours ;
They run up to my knees,
  Laughing and waving flowers.

They run up to my knees,
   They shout and cry Cuckoo!
They mock the bleating lambs,
   And like young calves they moo.

Some of their flowers are weeds,
   Are weeds, and nothing more;
But sweeter far they smell
   Than roses at my door.

It is a merry crew,
   And I curse Time that he
Has made me what I am—
   A man and mystery.

The Sea

HER cheeks were white, her eyes were wild,
   Her heart was with her sea-gone child.
"Men say you know and love the sea?
It is ten days, my child left me;
Ten days, and still he doth not come,
And I am weary of my home."

I thought of waves that ran the deep
And flashed like rabbits, when they leap,
The white part of their tails; the glee
Of captains that take brides to sea,
And own the ships they steer; how seas
Played leapfrog over ships with ease.

The great Sea-Wind, so rough and kind ;
Ho, ho ! his strength ; the great Sea-Wind
Blows iron tons across the sea !
Ho, ho ! his strength ; how wild and free !
He breaks the waves, to our amaze,
Into ten thousand little sprays !

" Nay, have no fear " ; I laughed with joy,
" That you have lost a sea-gone boy ;
The Sea's wild horses, they are far
More safe than Land's tamed horses are ;
They kick with padded hoofs, and bite
With teeth that leave no marks in sight.

True, Waves will howl when, all day long
The Wind keeps piping loud and strong ;
For in ships' sails the wild Sea-Breeze
Pipes sweeter than your birds in trees ;
But have no fear "—I laughed with joy,
" That you have lost a sea-gone boy."

That night I saw ten thousand bones
Coffined in ships, in weeds and stones ;
Saw how the Sea's strong jaws could take
Big iron ships like rats to shake ;
Heard him still moan his discontent
For one man or a continent.

I saw that woman go from place
To place, hungry for her child's face ;
I heard her crying, crying, crying ;
Then, in a flash ! saw the Sea trying,
With savage joy, and efforts wild,
To smash his rocks with a dead child.

Vain Beauty

AH, what is Beauty but vain show—
 If nothing in the heart is sweet;
As oft the spider finds a moth—
 All wings and little meat.

Thy look as warm as Autumn's is,
 As false—both he and thou art cold;
Then, since thou art unkind and vain,
 Let thy true worth be told.

Worms form thy flesh, and 'tis that flesh
 Makes thee so beautiful to see;
When dying thou refuse them food,
 They'll help themselves to thee.

Thy laugh was falser than men-make
 Ere they in dreadful battle fall;
I found thee false, thy looks deceived
 Like short men that sit tall.

Beauty can make thy two lips red—
 But not thy voice sound soft and sweet;
Beauty made thy cheeks smooth, but gave
 Thine eyes no pleasant heat.

I see thee move like a vain horse
 Whose neck is archèd to his knee;
His head will soon drop there through age—
 And age will so bend thee.

Age with his frost will warn thee soon,
  And pinch and mark thee here and there;
Will dry thy lip, and dim thine eye,
  And pull out thy long hair.

The flowers that spread their charms too far
 ⹁ Must soon be served like common weeds;
With my respect love also died—
  No longer my heart bleeds.

Waiting

WHO can abide indoors this morn,
  Now sunny May is ten days born;
In his house caged, a moping thing,
When all the merry free birds sing?
It is a pleasant time, and all
The sky's so full of cloudlets small,
That white doth seem Heaven's natural hue,
And clouds themselves are painted blue.
Now lusty May doth grow and burst
Her bodice green; her hawthorn breast,
Breaking those laces once so tight,
Doth more than peep its lovely white.
Come forth, my Love, for Nature wears
This hour her bridal smile; she hears
Ten thousand bantering birds, as they
Do hop upon her blossomed way.
The Sun doth shine, all things rejoice;
The cows forget the milkmaid's voice;

Of gardeners flowers have little care,
The sheep care not where shepherds are,
Dewdrops are in the grass, and they
Are twenty times more bright than day ;
And if we look them close their rays
Will even make our own eyes daze ;
But from that red and fiery Sun
Some timid drops of dew have run
Down the green blades of grass, and found
At once a cool place underground ;
The birds sing at their high, sweet pitch,
And bees sing basso deep and rich.
May is Love's month : her flowers and voice
Call youth and maiden to rejoice,
And fill their hearts with Love's sweet pains ;
They meet with laughter in green lanes,
And then they turn to whispering,
Under the leaves where the birds sing.
Fie, fie, my love ; you wait too long
To hear that old, black kettle's song ;
He'll keep thee suffering long for him,
And a true lover for his whim   .
I've seen where you did stand last night,
Near the old stile : that spot is white
With daisies, and I swear, they were
Never in that green place before ;
But that those sweet flowers came to sight
Since we two parted there last night,
At sunset, when that western world
Had four green rainbows rimmed with gold.
You indoors when the skylark long
Has sung on high his matin song !
The humble bees, dressed in black cloth,
Like mourners for the dead, come forth

Waiting

With their false groans—for soon they'll stop
With red-faced flowers to drink a drop;
Until they are so tight with drink,
They must lie down awhile and think.
So quiet lie the Butterflies,
Some Bees can scarce believe their eyes,
But what they're Blossoms, lovelier far,
And sweeter than all others are.
But one black Bee did come along,
A big, black bully, fat and strong,
And saw my Lady Butterfly,
Who, dreaming sweet romance, did lie
Lazy on a red flower; and he,
Vexed she'd not toil like Ant or Bee,
Buzzed in her ears, and grumbled so—
She must at last arise and go.
Come, Love, and breathe on these small flowers,
So they may live a few more hours.
Had I been near, you had not ta'en
Sleep's second draught and drowsed again,
But waked for good at my first kiss—
As Phœbus made these flowers with his.
Young Buds are here, that wait to see
How you do part your lips for me,
Ere they ope theirs the least—who wait
Your coming, Love, which is so late.
We'll miss, when summer is no more,
The very weed that chokes a flower.
Alas! too soon the time must come
When leaves will fall, and birds be dumb;
And but red Robin's breast will show
How the late fruits and flowers did glow.
The leafy Elm, that now has made
For twenty kine a pleasant shade,

Will in its scraggy bones stand bare,
With not one leaf seen anywhere.
The Stream will take and bury one
By one, till Willow's leaves are gone ;
The Hedge—see how it dances now !
Will stand to its broad waist in snow.
Yet what care I ?   If I have thee,
'Twill still be summer time to me ;
Though no Sun shines, when you come forth
A light must fall across the earth.

THE END

Crown 8vo.   Canvas.   320 pages.   6s.

The Autobiography of
A Super-Tramp

BY

WILLIAM H. DAVIES

Author of "The Soul's Destroyer," "New Poems," etc.

With Eight-page Preface by

G. BERNARD SHAW

"Perhaps the most interesting light ever shed on the life of a tramp."—*Star.*

"One of the most remarkable human documents ever published."—*Morning Leader.*

"Mr. Davies has written a remarkable book, for which it would be hard to find a parallel in the vast vagrant literature of Europe."—*Daily News.*

"Open-air literature has few if any books so delightful to read as this."—*Scotsman.*

"The autobiography of a poet like Mr. Davies was bound to be good."—*Daily Chronicle.*

"Certain to be widely read."—*Daily Mail.*

"A book of extraordinary interest to the reader and of extraordinary importance to the community."—*Observer.*

"We think Mr. Shaw is not far wrong when he calls this 'a most remarkable autobiography.'"—*Evening Standard.*

"Is too good not to be believed. It is an astonishing narrative, introduced by Mr. Shaw in an astonishing preface. . . . His book ought to be read by every adult too old and respectable to turn beggar. It is absorbingly real, and written with a self-knowledge and self-revelation that are irresistible."—*Globe.*

The Way of All Flesh. A Novel. New Edition. 6

Erewhon. A Satire. 11th Impression. 2s. 6d. net

Erewhon Re-visited. 3rd Issue. 2s. 6d. net

Essays on Life, Art, & Science. 2nd Issue. 2s. 6d. net

"The re-issue of these books gives ground for the hope th a very notable mind is about to enter into its kingdom. Th public has no longer any excuse for not knowing anything abo the most penetrating, honest, courageous and original of the criti of modern English life, the most detached and unacademic contributors to the literature of evolution. Mr. Birrell said r word too much in calling *Erewhon* the best satire of its kin since *Gulliver's Travels*. We venture to prophesy that in yea to come journalists will be referring to the Erewhonian ethi and system of life in general with almost as much confidence being understood as they have when they refer to anything i Sir W. S. Gilbert's works to-day. However, the day may l distant, for Butler wrote only for people who have learned to u: their minds. His greatest work was his posthumous nove *The Way of All Flesh*—a study of modern English life an character, more withering, because more true and restraine than anything penned by his famous disciple, Mr. Shaw."—*T Outlook, April* 25, 1908.

"Samuel Butler was, in his own department, the greate English writer of the latter half of the nineteenth century. drives one almost to despair of English literature when one se so extraordinary a study of English life as *The Way of All Fle* making so little stir that when, some years later, I produce pla in which Butler's extraordinarily fresh free and future piercin suggestions have an obvious share, I am met with nothing b vague cacklings about Ibsen and Nietzsche."—*Bernard Shaw, i preface to Major Barbara.*

"Many will welcome a cheaper edition of the works of th very original writer . . . and it will help to give them the wide publicity which they deserve."—*The Times.*

"We have often dwelt upon the remarkable originality an freshness of Butler as a thinker. He is not for all minds, bi those who know his powers will agree with Mr. Shaw's heart tribute."—*Athenæum.*

London : A. C. Fifield, 44 Fleet Street, E.C